THE AUTHENTIC JAPANESE COOKBOOK

70 CLASSIC AND MODERN RECIPES MADE EASY | TAKE AT HOME TRADITIONAL AND MODERN DISHES MADE SIMPLE FOR CONTEMPORARY TASTES.

JAMIE WOODS

CONTENTS

Introduction   vii

INTRODUCTION TO JAPANESE CUISINE
History of Japanese Cuisine   3
Traditional History of Japanese Dishes   5
Health Benefits of Japanese Food   7
Key Ingredients to Prepare Japanese Dishes   9

JAPANESE BREAKFAST AND SNACK RECIPES
1. Vegan Japanese Souffle Pancakes   13
2. Homemade Senbei Rice Crackers   15
3. Japanese Rice Balls   17
4. Cucumber Sunomono   19
5. Tofu Hiyayakko   20
6. Japanese Breakfast Porridge Bowl   21
7. Japanese Beef Tataki Rolls   23
8. Pancakes Dorayaki   25
9. Tamagoyaki Scramble   27
10. Japanese Natto   29
11. Salmon Cucumber Tartare Bites   30
12. Teriyaki Mushroom Bowl   32
13. Japanese Ogura Toast   34
14. Vegetable Lo Mein   35

JAPANESE LUNCH, SALAD, AND SOUP RECIPES
15. Okonomiyaki   39
16. Aji Nanbanzuke Spicy Horse Mackerel with Vegetables   41
17. Miso Soup with Tofu, Wakame Seaweed   43
18. Japanese Shrimp & Eggplant Fried Rice   45
19. Egg-and-Miso Soup   47

20. Mashed Tofu Salad with Green Bean	48
21. Katsu Curry	50
22. BBQ Pork Chashu	51
23. Japanese Rice Balls with Avocado Filling	53
24. Somen Noodles with Nori Dressing	55
25. Unagi Hitsumabushi Grilled Eel Rice Bowl	57
26. Japanese Udon Noodle Soup	59
27. Hot Pot with Miso	61
28. Japanese Coco Ichibanya-Style Vegetable Curry	63
29. Yakitori Grilled Skewers	65
30. Karaage Japanese Fried Chicken	67

JAPANESE DINNER AND DESSERTS RECIPES

31. Tamago Kake Gohan	71
32. Lightly Fried Japanese Vegetables	72
33. Vegetable Gyoza	74
34. Tofu Katsu with Spicy Sweet-Sour Sauce	76
35. Japanese Vegetable Stew with Miso Broth	78
36. 15 Minute Spicy Udon	80
37. Japanese Miso Eggplant	82
38. No-Bake Crème Caramel	84
39. Vegetable Yakisoba	86
40. Szechuan Eggplant	88
41. Japanese Fruit Sandwich	90
42. Strawberry Mochi	92

MOST FAMOUS JAPANESE DISHES

43. Japanese Mitarashi Dango	97
44. Creamy Miso Pasta with Tofu and Asparagus	99
45. Wagamama Wok-Fried Greens	101
46. Japanese Soba Noodles	103
47. Soy-Glazed Eggplant Donburi	105
48. Japanese Mushroom Stir-Fry	107
49. Japanese Shiitake and Vegetable Rice	109
50. Spicy Tofu Bento Bowl	111
51. Yasai Itame	113
52. Lightly Fried Japanese Vegetables	115
53. Hearty Vegetable Miso Soup	117

54. Kurigohan (Chestnut Rice)	118
55. Japanese Stir-Fried Noodles with Veggies	120
56. Hibachi Vegetables	122

JAPANESE RAMEN AND SUSHI RECIPES

57. Vegetarian Ramen	127
58. Instant Pot Ramen Recipe	129
59. Tonkatsu Ramen Soup	131
60. Chicken Ramen	132
61. Savory Mushroom and Vegetable Ramen Soup	134
62. Spicy Vegetarian Ramen	136
63. Rich and Creamy Tonkotsu Ramen Broth Recipe	138
64. Nigirizushi	140
65. Sushi Rice	141
66. Chawanmushi	143
67. Kitsune Udon	145
68. Cutlet Rice Bowl Katsudon	147
69. California Sushi Rolls	149
70. Sushi Bake California Maki	151

Conclusion	153

© **Copyright 2021 by Jamie Woods- All rights reserved.**

This document is geared towards providing exact and reliable information in regards to the topic and issue covered. The publication is sold with the idea that the publisher is not required to render accounting, officially permitted, or otherwise, qualified services. If advice is necessary, legal or professional, a practiced individual in the profession should be ordered.

- From a Declaration of Principles which was accepted and approved equally by a Committee of the American Bar Association and a Committee of Publishers and Associations.

It is not legal in any way to reproduce, duplicate, or transmit any part of this document in either electronic means or in printed format. Recording of this publication is strictly prohibited and any storage of this document is not allowed unless with written permission from the publisher. All rights reserved.

The information provided herein is stated to be truthful and consistent, in that any liability, in terms of inattention or otherwise, by any usage or abuse of any policies, processes, or directions contained within is the solitary and utter responsibility of the recipient reader. Under no circumstances will any legal responsibility or blame be held against the publisher for any reparation, damages, or monetary loss due to the information herein, either directly or indirectly.

Respective authors own all copyrights not held by the publisher.

The information herein is offered for informational purposes solely, and is universal as so. The presentation of the information is without contract or any type of guarantee assurance.

The trademarks that are used are without any consent, and the publication of the trademark is without permission or backing by the trademark owner. All trademarks and brands within this book are for clarifying purposes only and are the owned by the owners themselves, not affiliated with this document.

INTRODUCTION

Each food is named "Gohan." by the Japanese. For instance, breakfast is called "asa-Gohan." In traditional Japanese dishes, a cup of boiled rice is also included and may be a component of dinner, breakfast, or lunch. The side dishes are known as okazu and are eaten with broth and rice. While Japan is a small world, each area and even town has its distinct flavor. Food from the Kanto areas (the eastern part of the big island) and the Kansai area (the western part of the big island) are the most popular. Kanto cuisine is known for its bold flavors, while Kansai cuisine is known for its soft seasoning. Many dishes in the Kansai and Kanto areas are prepared differently. Traditional Japanese meals involve a cup of fried rice, which can be eaten for breakfast, noon, or supper.

    Perfect arrangement, pure flavors, and specialty foods are the hallmarks of Japanese cuisine. Meals are ornate affairs steeped in tradition and ritual, with a variety of main courses served alongside boiled vegetables, pickles, and spice mixes– all offered in specially selected individual bowls. It is easy to see why when you look at Japan's environment. Encircled by the ocean, Japan's chain of mountainous islands is crisscrossed by rivers, and it was

Introduction

from these plentiful waterways that the Japanese captured fresh seafood, which is the centerpiece of most Japanese dinners.

Without a doubt, Japan has become one of the world's great food countries. New seasonal harvest and gentle preparation are the key components of Japanese cuisine. Japanese cuisine has exploded into the culinary scene. It's no surprise that Japanese cuisine is so common, given its mastery of flavors and delicate balance of sweet and savory. Japanese and Japanese-inspired foods can be found worldwide, even in the local kitchen, mainly seafood and ramen. Water is also at the heart of Japanese food, with dashi made from Kombu (kelp) and bonito particles in water serving as the basis for all Japanese sauces. The essence of Japanese cuisine is new, seasonal flavors cooked simply in water. As a result, it carries the "healthy" label well.

With these extinct flavors, "Japanese Cookbook" has a wide range of delicious Japanese recipes. It has six chapters with appetizers, snacks, breakfast, lunch, dinner, desserts, and Japan's most famous recipes. There is also a focus on sushi and ramen recipes. Read this book, follow these recipes, and have a flavorful, delicious meal every day.

INTRODUCTION TO JAPANESE CUISINE

With a boundless array of local and regional foods, Japanese cuisine promises an assortment of gastronomic pleasures. There is a wide selection of dishes and ethnic specializations of Japanese food. Japan is broken into different regional areas, each of which has formed its distinctive culinary traditions. Consequently, as they pass from place to place, travelers may experience a varied range of national foods.

Japanese food has taken the horticultural environment by storm. With its unique skill of flavorings and a sensitive mixture of salty and sweet, it is no wonder Japanese ingredients are so common. From ramen to sushi, dishes influenced by Japanese and Japanese could be seen anywhere, such as your country's restaurants! To take home the magnificent ingredients of Japanese food, you do not need to be a professional chef.

HISTORY OF JAPANESE CUISINE

Japanese food has been affected by other civilizations' food practices, but it has adapted and modified to establish its distinctive form of preparing food behaviors. About 300 B.C., China was the very first foreign intervention in Japan. When they learned to raise rice from the Japanese. China was also responsible for using utensils and soybean curd production (tofu), and soy sauce.

Trade with the rest of the countries started introducing foreign ideas to Japan starting in the early 13th century. The Dutch brought bread, cabbage, and sweet potatoes. The Spanish established tempura. During the Meiji Era, the meat went to Japan after a prohibition of even more than thousands of years. During the late 20th century, Modern items, such as coffee, bread, and frozen yogurt, became popular. The adoption of time-saving cooking techniques has become another Westernization.

Japanese food is associated with better food and has a deep relationship with the region's long-expected lifespan. One of the key factors behind all this is 'ichijyusansa' that applies to a meal composed of brown rice and broth, the main dish of fish or meat, and a fresh salad of vegetables or seaweed, all slightly flavored to display the components' natural flavors.

TRADITIONAL HISTORY OF JAPANESE DISHES

Rice arrived from Korea, wheat and soybean came from China and a crucial Japanese cuisine component. In Britain, yogurt and other dairy products have struggled to enjoy the same success as In Japan. Between both the eighth and fifteenth generations, the only Japanese dairy material documented in history was made. It was also just for pulling carts or plowing fields that cattle were bred. It was, until quite lately, a long-forgotten tradition to use them for beef or even dairy.

Fish was an important replacement in the lack of beef. As both an island nation, this food source was plentiful and inspired many of the world's most common dishes before modern distribution methods were adopted. However, the complexity of storing and shipping fresh aquatic fish reduced consumption in inland areas because aquatic fish are widely consumed.

Wasabi is among the globe's most challenging ingredients to produce, and that is why the crop is so pricey. Many wasabis in cafes are usually horseradish combined with food dye processing for this purpose. True wasabi has a more herbal taste than the artificial type, but it lacks its punch for about fifteen minutes after being diced.

HEALTH BENEFITS OF JAPANESE FOOD

The Japanese diet is focused on long-term health philosophy. Japanese cuisine is not only delicious and enticing, but it also has several health advantages. Uncooked meats, added sugars or foods, and a lot of fruit and legumes are all part of traditional Japanese cuisine. Hormone-dependent tumors, such as breast and cervical cancer, have historically been rare in Japan. This is due to a higher intake of vegetables, berries, good fats, high-fiber products, and a lower calorie consumption overall. Japan has one of the lowest levels of cardiovascular disease development globally and even lower compared to developing countries. The Japanese diet is full of foods that help support heart health, which explains why there are very few cases of heart disease. Green tea, which has various health benefits, is commonly served with Japanese dishes. Green tea has been shown to help lower blood pressure, strengthen the immune system, lower blood pressure, and delay the aging process.

KEY INGREDIENTS TO PREPARE JAPANESE DISHES

Here are some of the main ingredients to prepare Japanese cuisine at home:
- Soy sauce
- Noodles
- Wasabi
- Shichimi togarashi
- Nori
- Rice vinegar
- Bonito flakes
- Kombu
- Mirin
- Miso paste
- Wakame
- Sushi rice

Japanese dishes have carefully balanced flavors, but the flavorings that give them their complexity are typically made from the same ingredients.

JAPANESE BREAKFAST AND SNACK RECIPES

1

VEGAN JAPANESE SOUFFLE PANCAKES

Cooking Time: 20 minutes
Serving Size: 2
Ingredients:
Dry Ingredients
- ¼ teaspoon baking soda
- Pinch of salt
- 1 tablespoon sugar
- 1 teaspoon baking powder
- 80g all-purpose flour

Wet Ingredients
- 2 teaspoons oil
- 1 teaspoon vanilla extract
- 1 tablespoon apple cider vinegar
- 80ml soy milk

Method:

1. Lubricate the appropriately with oil or vegetarian butter when you're using ring molds.
2. Mix the flour mixture very well in a pan.
3. Shift the flour mixture on the one hand and insert the apple cider vinegar, vanilla extract, plant-based milk, and oil.

4. Slowly pour together all the products until no dry patches remain. Do not spill over.

5. Over the moderate fire, heat a wide skillet.

6. Transfer a thin film of oil to the rim. Turn the heat down to moderate when the oil is hot.

7. Position the molds of the ring so that among them, there seems to be some room.

8. Twice, the batter is spooned under one mold, then the other.

9. Now scoop the batter into two large piles when you're not using a mold. Use a lid to protect the pot and let it heat for ten minutes.

10. The surfaces of the cakes should never be shiny for more than ten minutes.

11. They must have some wrinkles on the horizon, and that they should appear dry on the bottom. Switch the pancakes using a spatula.

12. However, place the bowl once more and cook for the next three minutes before the pancakes are cooked fully.

13. Remove and expose the bowl from the flame.

14. Serve with a vegetarian oil or a coconut whip and golden syrup instantly.

2

HOMEMADE SENBEI RICE CRACKERS

Cooking Time: 40 minutes
Serving Size: 4
Ingredients:
Senbei
- 2 tablespoon vegetable oil
- 4 tablespoon water
- 40g cooked white rice
- ¼ teaspoon sea salt
- 120g rice flour or mochiko

Glaze
- 2 teaspoon mirin
- 1 tablespoon soy sauce

Toppings
- 2 teaspoon red chili pepper mix
- Nori seaweed sheets
- 3 teaspoon black sesame seeds
- 5 teaspoon furikake rice

Method:
1. Preheat the oven to 190 degrees Celsius.
2. To make the glaze, whisk together the soy sauce and mirin.

3. In a mixing bowl, combine the corn starch, rice flour, salt, and oil to produce the pastry.

4. Run until the mixture is finely mixed.

5. Place the mixture in a bowl and insert your desired flavorings.

6. Remove the plastic from the dough 'disc' and place it on the prepared baking sheet.

7. Bake the pretzels for 8-10 minutes, one baking tray at a time.

8. Using a spatula, turn the pretzels.

9. Bake for 8-10 minutes more, or until the crackers begin to tan.

10. Brush the soy sauce and miso glaze over the tops.

11. Return to the oven and bake for another ten minutes or until well browned.

12. Before serving, cool full on a wire rack.

3
JAPANESE RICE BALLS

Cooking Time: 1 hour
Serving Size: 4
Ingredients:
- 1 teaspoon toasted sesame oil
- ½ avocado
- ½ teaspoon salt
- ½ – 1 small sweet potato
- 2 tablespoon rice wine vinegar
- 1 tablespoon sugar
- 3 cups water
- ¼ cup sesame seeds
- 1 ½ cup brown sushi rice

Teriyaki Sauce
- 2 tablespoons sugar
- 1 tablespoon rice wine vinegar
- 5 tablespoons soy sauce
- 5 tablespoons mirin
- Vegetable oil for frying

Method:
1. Begin by doing the rice cleaning.

2. Quantify the rice into the pan and wash it with cool water several times till the water no longer looks murky and begins to appear clean. Drain some rice.

3. Use ice water to coat the rice, put the pot on the flame, and protect it with a cover. Switch the heat off when the water heats.

4. Offer it a stirring and allow the water to consume the rice.

5. The rice must be weak after thirty minutes. Drain all water in bulk.

6. Strip a large mixing bowl with films from the kitchen and drop around one tablespoon of cooled rice in it.

7. Preheat the frying pan and pour some oil over it.

8. Fry Onigiri over medium temperature until crisp and well caramelized, three minutes per hand. Serve with teriyaki sauce instantly.

9. Integrate the soya sauce, vinegar, mirin, and sugar in a shallow saucepan.

10. Bring it to the boil with the gravy. Blend the corn starch with liquid in a tiny cup.

11. Steadily dump the corn starch combination into the sauce when continuously stirring it.

12. Continue cooking until you have caramelized the sauce. Switch the heat off over the pan.

4

CUCUMBER SUNOMONO

Cooking Time: 1 hour 15 minutes
Serving Size: 5
Ingredients:
- 1 teaspoon salt
- 1 ½ teaspoons ginger root
- ⅓ cup rice vinegar
- 4 teaspoons white sugar
- 2 large cucumbers, peeled

Method:

1. Cucumbers should be split in half lengthwise, and any big seeds should be scooped out.
2. Cut into very small pieces crosswise.
3. Combine the vinegar, starch, salt, and seasoning in a shallow cup. Mix well.
4. Put cucumbers in the cup and swirl to cover them with the solution evenly.
5. Before eating, chill the cucumber dish for at least 1 hour.

5
TOFU HIYAYAKKO

Cooking Time: 10 minutes
Serving Size: 1
Ingredients:
- 1 pinch bonito shavings
- 1 pinch toasted sesame seeds
- 1 ½ teaspoon fresh ginger root
- ¼ teaspoon green onion
- 1 tablespoon soy sauce
- ½ teaspoon water
- ¼ (12 ounces) package silken tofu
- ½ teaspoon dashi granules
- 1 teaspoon white sugar

Method:

1. In a shallow bowl, blend the sugar, dashi granules, soy sauce, and water when the sugar is dissolved.

2. On a small dish, put the tofu and cover it with green onion, ginger, and bonito granules.

3. Sprinkle on top of the soy combination and scatter with sesame seeds.

6
JAPANESE BREAKFAST PORRIDGE BOWL

Cooking Time: 10 minutes
Serving Size: 1
Ingredients:
- 20g of firm
- Water for desired consistency
- 1 tablespoon nutritional yeast
- ¼ of a small avocado
- 20g round brown rice (dry)
- 1 nori sheet, shredded
- 1 teaspoon miso paste
- ½ cup chopped leek
- 20g rolled oats

To Garnish
- Sesame seeds
- Paprika powder

Method:
1. Begin by draining brown rice. Wash and clean.
2. Place the rolled oats in a shallow saucepan in the morning before preparing the porridge, then add only enough hot water to fill them. Just put aside.

3. You could either rip the nori papers with your palms or cut them with knives.

4. Then, cook the soaked rice and the sliced leek in a room temperature water frying pan till the rice is ready, about ten minutes.

5. Turn the heating off. Then, blend in the soaking rolled oats and insert the appropriate boiling water.

6. Then, combine some liquid with miso paste and switch things up with ripped nori paper and nutritional yeast into the mixture.

7. Again, when necessary, add a little water.

7
JAPANESE BEEF TATAKI ROLLS

Cooking Time: 20 minutes
Serving Size: 24 rolls
Ingredients:
- 2 teaspoon sesame seeds
- Large bunch cilantro
- 1 green
- 2 red chilies
- ¼ napa cabbage
- 1 carrot
- 1 lb. beef filet
- 1 tablespoon sesame oil
- 1 teaspoon sugar
- 4 tablespoon soy sauce
- 1 tablespoon neutral oil

Method:

1. Warm a nonstick or sheet iron frying pan over medium temperature until it is smoking hot.

2. Sear the beef fillet for 40 seconds on either side after brushing it with the neutral spray.

3. In a small cup, combine the sesame oil, soy sauce, glucose, and whisk until the sugar has melted.

4. Transfer two tablespoons of the seasoning to the meat and rub it on.

5. Save the remaining dressing for the day.

6. Refrigerate the meat for at least an hour after wrapping it in glad tape.

7. Thinly slice the napa lettuce, cabbage, spring onions, and red chili.

8. Slice the beef finely and place a portion of each vegetable in the center.

9. Sprinkle a little of the coating on each roll before gently rolling it up.

10. Serve hot with sesame seeds.

8
PANCAKES DORAYAKI

Cooking Time: 20 minutes
Serving Size: 2
Ingredients:
- Vegetable oil
- ½ cup red bean paste
- 2 tablespoon mirin or maple syrup
- ¼ teaspoon soy sauce
- ½ cup sifted cake flour
- 2 teaspoon baking powder
- ⅓ cup soy milk
- 2 tablespoon powdered sugar

Method:
1. In a large cup, mix the flour, icing sugar, and cornstarch.
2. Add the maple syrup, soy milk, and soy sauce to some other dish.
3. To form a delicious mixture, drop the dried mixture into the wet one, and mix.
4. It is not meant to be so dense, but this should be small enough just to pour. For ten minutes, let everything sit.

5. In a non-stick pan or pot, pour that small amount of oil and warm it over moderate flame.

6. To disperse the oil equally, use a towel. You just want the slightest amount to help shade the pancakes but not adhere to them.

7. Reduce heat to medium, and dump about two tablespoons of the batter in as ideal the round as you can find on the non-stick plate.

8. You need all of them to be approximately the same number.

9. For around two minutes, heat on the first hand, bubbles might rise on edge, and the sides will cook very easily.

10. For around one more minute, turn and heat on the other hand.

11. Enable your cakes to chill for several minutes, then add a dollop of Anko, the bean paste, to each of them.

12. To make the Dorayaki, cover it with a croissant and stack it all together.

13. Serve with a swirl of icing sugar or cream cheese or diced strawberries with almond.

9
TAMAGOYAKI SCRAMBLE

Cooking Time: 3 minutes
Serving Size: 1
Ingredients:
- ¼ teaspoon black salt
- pepper to taste
- 2 teaspoon sugar (10g)
- ⅛ teaspoon baking powder
- ½ teaspoon kombu dashi
- 2 teaspoon mirin (10g)
- 1 sheet yuba
- 3 tablespoon liquid of choice
- 1 teaspoon soy sauce
- ¼ cup silken tofu (60g)

Garnish
- Scallions
- Sesame seeds
- Kizami nori
- Soy sauce

Optional
- 1 tablespoon vegan kewpie mayo

- Pinch of turmeric
- 2 teaspoon nutritional yeast (8g)

Method:

1. Moisturize in warm water for 3-5 minutes, dry yuba.
2. Rip the yuba into smaller parts, about around the size of a fist.
3. Mix soy milk, silken tofu, mirin, soy sauce, rice, dashi, sugar, and baking powder thoroughly together.
4. This is going to be the eggy mixture, which shuffles as well.
5. Over medium-high heat, warm a bowl, and add oils or vegetarian butter.
6. Add the silken tofu and put the yuba stuff on top. Before handling it, let it cook for around two minutes.
7. Use spoons or a spatula until the sides start to look fried, then force the sides into the center.
8. Lower the heat and simmer for another thirty seconds, moving the egg mixture to the right texture every few minutes.
9. Squeeze the black salt on the edge using your fingertips.
10. Take it out of the oven and eat on the sides or over pasta.

10

JAPANESE NATTO

Cooking Time: 5 minutes
Serving Size: 1
Ingredients:
- 1 teaspoon soy sauce
- 3 shiso leaves
- Steamed Rice
- 1 tablespoon Katsuobushi bonito flakes
- Japanese yellow mustard
- 1 tablespoon green onions
- 1 package Natto

Method:
1. Combine all the components, excluding the shiso and steamed rice.
2. Mix very well until it is dense.
3. Place the rice around and line it with Shiso.

11

SALMON CUCUMBER TARTARE BITES

Cooking Time: 50 minutes
  Serving Size: 4
Ingredients:
For Serving
- Finely minced scallions
- Black sesame seeds optional
- Japanese seven flavor chili pepper
- 1 English cucumber

Salmon Tartare
- 1 teaspoon mirin
- ½ teaspoon sesame oil
- 2 teaspoons scallions
- 1 teaspoon soy sauce
- ½ pound fresh salmon fillet

Method:

1. Combine the salmon, green onions, sesame oil, mirin, and soy sauce in a medium mixing dish.
2. Cucumber ends should be trimmed.
3. Use a knife, score the cucumber skin laterally.

4. To serve, spoon Salmon Tartare into cucumber circles and marinade with Ichimi Togarashi and white sesame seeds.

5. Serve right away.

12

TERIYAKI MUSHROOM BOWL

Cooking Time: 45 minutes
Serving Size: 4
Ingredients:
- 2 tablespoon sesame seeds
- 2-3 scallions, sliced thinly
- 1 teaspoon red chili flakes
- 1 lb. broccolini, about 12 stalks
- 1 cup dry brown rice
- 2 garlic cloves, finely minced
- 2 teaspoon ginger, minced
- 6 Portobello mushrooms
- 1 tablespoon white miso paste
- 1 tablespoon brown sugar
- 3 tablespoon soy sauce
- 2 tablespoon rice vinegar
- 3 tablespoon sesame oil

Method:
1. Heat the flame to 425 degrees F.
2. Slice the mushrooms and cover them with 1 tablespoon of sesame oil.

3.Switch to a cookie dish and bake until the mushroom is soft and the liquid flows for twenty minutes, rotating halfway across.

4.Cook rice as per the instructions in the box.

5.In the meantime, in a small shallow saucepan, mix the brown sugar, rice vinegar, soy sauce, ginger, garlic, and chili powder.

6.Heat till the sugar dissolves, and the paste gets thicker into a coating, stirring regularly.

7.To smooth it out, if you moisten this too much, put in 1 tablespoon of water.

8.Shave the woody edges off the broccolini and sprinkle on a cookie dish with the leftover two tablespoons of sesame oil and salt season.

9.Pull them from the cooker until the mushroom is baked.

10.With both the teriyaki coating, coat all parts of the mushroom and the red cabbage.

11.Put the broccolini and mushroom back in the oven for ten minutes before the broccolini is the saddle and the mushrooms are caramelized.

12.Spray with sesame oil and clear everything from the cooker.

13.For a side dish, serve broccoli and mushroom over rice and finish with spring onions.

13

JAPANESE OGURA TOAST

Cooking Time: 13 minutes
Serving Size: 8
Ingredients:
- Margarine or butter
- 8 tablespoon whipped cream
- 8 tablespoon red bean paste
- 2 pieces white bread

Method:

1. Butter the white bread by cutting it into fourths and toasting it until crispy.

2. While the toast is still sweet, spread real cheese or butter on it.

3. On each bread square, spread one tablespoon bean paste powder and one tablespoon cream cheese.

14

VEGETABLE LO MEIN

Cooking Time: 25 minutes
Serving Size: 4
Ingredients:
- ½ cup snow peas
- 3 cups baby spinach
- 1 red bell pepper
- 1 carrot
- 8 ounces egg noodles
- 2 cloves garlic
- 2 cups cremini mushrooms
- 1 tablespoon olive oil

For the Sauce
- ½ teaspoon ground ginger
- ½ teaspoon Sriracha
- 2 teaspoons sugar
- 1 teaspoon sesame oil
- 2 tablespoons soy sauce

Method:
1. Set down a bowl full containing sesame oil, sugar, soy sauce, spice, and Sriracha.

2. Heat pasta as per package directions in a large pot of water; rinse well.

3. In a medium saucepan or skillet, heat the olive oil over medium heat.

4. Garlic, onions, red pepper, and carrot are added to the pan.

5. Mix in the green beans and spinach for around 2-3 minutes, or until the kale has ripened.

6. Toss in the egg noodles with the soy sauce combination and toss gently to blend.

7. Serve right away.

JAPANESE LUNCH, SALAD, AND SOUP RECIPES

15

OKONOMIYAKI

Cooking Time: 30 minutes
Serving Size: 2
Ingredients:
- 2 spring onions, thinly sliced
- 1 tablespoon oil
- 120 grams shredded green cabbage
- 1 small carrot, grated
- ½ teaspoon pureed ginger
- Black pepper
- 4 eggs
- 1 tablespoon soy sauce
- 80 grams plain flour

To Serve
- Chopped spring onions
- Sesame seeds
- Sriracha
- Mayonnaise or salad cream

Method:
1. In a blending pan, beat the eggs and then insert the flour.
2. Mix to shape the mixture for the pancake.

3. Include the pureed ginger and soy sauce, lots of black pepper, then insert the carrot, cabbage, and spring onions that are finely chopped.

4. Heat for several minutes over medium-high heat.

5. Repeat to make four pancakes in sum with the leftover pancake combination.

16

AJI NANBANZUKE SPICY HORSE MACKEREL WITH VEGETABLES

Cooking Time: 2 hours
Serving Size: 2-3
Ingredients:
- Pinch of salt and pepper
- Oil for frying
- 2 bell peppers
- 3 tablespoon potato starch
- 1 onion
- 1 carrot
- 3 horse mackerel fillets

For the Marinade
- 1 ½ tablespoon soy sauce
- 1 red chili pepper
- 1 tablespoon mirin rice wine
- 1 tablespoon sake
- 50ml sushi vinegar

Method:
1. Red chili peppers can be cut into small rounds.
2. Merge all of the marinade ingredients in a mixing bowl and set aside.

3. Any of the veggies should be thinly sliced.
4. Place a small amount of oil in a deep fryer.
5. Sauté the veggies before they are tender and soft.
6. Remove the pan from the fire and insert the marinade, tossing gently.
7. Season the fillets on both sides with salt and pepper.
8. After that, gently coat in corn starch.
9. Preheat any cooking oil to 180°C in a frying pan.
10. Carefully place 1-2 fillets at the moment, skins down flat, into the oil, and cook until crispy.
11. Position the fillets on a pan, then spill the veggies and marinade over them.
12. For a complete dinner, serve with rice.

17

MISO SOUP WITH TOFU, WAKAME SEAWEED

Cooking Time: 15 minutes
Serving Size: 2
Ingredients:
- ½ cup chopped green onion
- ¼ cup firm tofu
- 3-4 tablespoon yellow miso paste
- ½ cup chopped green chard
- 1 sheet nori
- 4 cups vegetable broth

Method:

1. In a small mixing bowl, put the vegetable broth and take it to a low boil.

2. Meanwhile, place the miso in a shallow saucepan, add a little more warm water, and swirl until soft.

3. When transferred to the broth later, this would guarantee that it does not clump. Just put aside.

4. Transfer chard, spring onions, and tofu to the liquid and cook for five minutes.

5. Insert nori, next, and mix. Add the miso solution, detach from the flame, and whisk to blend.

6. When desired, try and add additional miso or a touch of kosher salt.

7. Serve it warm. It is better when clean.

18

JAPANESE SHRIMP & EGGPLANT FRIED RICE

Cooking Time: 35 minutes
Serving Size: 4
Ingredients:
- 2 cups brown rice
- ¼ cup ponzu sauce
- 2 cups eggplant
- 1 cup shelled edamame
- 2 teaspoons garlic
- 1 pound raw shrimp
- 3 scallions
- 2 teaspoons ginger
- 2 large eggs
- 1 teaspoon peanut oil

Method:
1. In a big flat-bottomed wok, warm 1 teaspoon oil.
2. Heat without mixing the eggs.
3. 1 tablespoon oil, green onions, garlic, and cloves in a skillet; cook, swirling, once scallions are soft.
4. Cook for two minutes, stirring constantly.
5. Cook the eggplant and edamame together.

6. Fill a big plate halfway with the contents of the skillet.

7. In the same wok, add the rest one tablespoon oil; add the rice and swirl until it is sweet.

8. Transfer the seafood, vegetables, and shells to the skillet, along with the ponzu sauce, and stir properly.

19

EGG-AND-MISO SOUP

Cooking Time: 20 minutes
Serving Size: 1
Ingredients:
- Chopped scallions
- Coarse salt and ground pepper
- 1 large egg
- 1 cup baby spinach
- 2 tablespoons white miso

Method:

1. In a skillet, put 1 ½ cups of water on the stove. Mix until it disperses fully in miso.

2. Put the eggs softly in a tiny bag, then slip them softly into the simmering liquid.

3. Cook for about two minutes before the whites are just fixed, and the yolk is still watery.

4. Add spinach and steam for about two minutes, until softened.

5. Spray with spring onions and add salt and black pepper to spice.

20

MASHED TOFU SALAD WITH GREEN BEAN

Cooking Time: 30 minutes
   Serving Size: 2
Ingredients:
- 9 oz. green beans
- 7 oz. silken tofu

Seasonings
- 1 teaspoon soy sauce
- ⅛ teaspoon kosher salt
- 1 tablespoon sugar
- 2 teaspoon miso
- 4 tablespoon white sesame seeds

Method:
1. Collect all the products.
2. On a sheet or pan, place the sealed tofu.
3. On top of the tofu, place another plate or tray and carry a massive item on top to allow drainage. Place thirty minutes free.
4. Put to a boil a huge pot of boiling water.
5. Boil up the crisp-tender green beans.
6. Well, rinse and put aside.
7. Break the green beans into small bits horizontally.

8. Pour in the soy sauce and mix them around. For later, put aside.

9. In a cooking pot, roast the sesame seeds, constantly tossing the wok.

10. Use the hands to split it into bits and transfer it to the sesame seed combination.

11. Tasting the tofu and seasoning with salts to taste is essential.

12. When mixed, you can cool for thirty minutes in the fridge before eating or serve instantly.

21

KATSU CURRY

Cooking Time: 15 minutes
  Serving Size: 2
Ingredients:
- 1 cup frozen stir fry vegetables
- Cooked rice
- 2 vegetarian schnitzels
- 1 block of Golden Curry

Method:
1. As advised, prepare the schnitzels or cutlets.
2. Break and set it aside into pieces.
3. Steam a pan and cook the veggies that are frozen.
4. To loosen the curry cube, insert the Golden Curry square, ½ cup of hot water, and mix.
5. Transfer a little extra water if the sauce gets too heavy.
6. Transfer the warm rice to a container to eat and put the bits of schnitzel on board.
7. Fill with the veggies and gravy and eat immediately.

22

BBQ PORK CHASHU

Cooking Time: 1 hour 20 minutes
Serving Size: 4-6
Ingredients:
- 2 pieces ginger
- 1 leek
- 110g sugar
- 2 cloves garlic
- 1.3kg pork belly
- 200ml cooking sake
- 50ml mirin
- 1-liter water
- 500ml soy sauce

Method:
1. Use the baker's rope, roll the pulled pork, leaving the skin on edge.
2. Parsley and spice can be roughly chopped and peeled.
3. Over low heat, combine the soy sauce, steam, boiling sake, mirin, honey, garlic, spice, and leek in a big pan.
4. After that, toss in the rolled pork belly.
5. Decrease to low, medium heat for 3-4 hours.

6. It is important to remember to boil it low and slow.

7. Allow cooling before marinating in the sauce night in the refrigerator.

8. Cover the pork with cling film after removing it from the liquid.

9. Serve ramen noodles, hot rice, or vegetables thinly sliced.

23

JAPANESE RICE BALLS WITH AVOCADO FILLING

Cooking Time: 1 hour
Serving Size: 4
Ingredients:
- 1 teaspoon toasted sesame oil
- ½ avocado
- ½ teaspoon salt
- ½ – 1 small sweet potato
- 2 tablespoon rice wine vinegar
- 1 tablespoon sugar
- 3 cups water
- ¼ cup sesame seeds
- 1 ½ cup brown sushi rice

Teriyaki Sauce
- 2 tablespoons sugar
- 1 tablespoon rice wine vinegar
- 5 tablespoons soy sauce
- 5 tablespoons mirin
- Vegetable oil for frying

Method:
13. Begin by doing the rice cleaning.

14. Use ice water to coat the rice, put the pot on the flame, and protect it with a cover. Switch the heat off when the water heats.

15. Offer it a stirring and allow the water to consume the rice.

16. Strip a large mixing bowl with films from the kitchen and drop around one tablespoon of cooled rice in it.

17. With certain rice, surround the stuffing and push it into a standardized ball.

18. Continue cooking until you have caramelized the sauce. Switch the heat off over the pan.

24

SOMEN NOODLES WITH NORI DRESSING

Cooking Time: 1 hour
Serving Size: 2
Ingredients:
For the Noodles
- 2 packages of somen noodles

For the Seaweed Dressing
- ½ teaspoon sesame oil
- A pinch of salt
- 2-3 tablespoons sesame seeds
- 1 teaspoon sugar
- 2 sheets of nori

For the Sauce
- 2 tablespoons sesame oil
- A splash of maple syrup
- 2-3 tablespoons rice vinegar
- 2-3 tablespoons tamarind

Method:
1. Cook the pasta as per the directions provided in the box.
2. Mix all the components for the sauces and set them aside.

3.Combine and set it aside from the components for the seaweed coating.

4.Break the pasta into two cups.

5.Place over the sauces and marinade with the toppings you like. Just serve.

25

UNAGI HITSUMABUSHI GRILLED EEL RICE BOWL

Cooking Time: 50 minutes
Serving Size: 1
Ingredients:
- Wasabi paste
- Dashi stock
- Shredded nori seaweed
- Chopped spring onions
- 1 grilled unagi eel filet
- Japanese sansho pepper powder
- 160g fresh steamed rice

Unagi Sauce
- 2 tablespoon soy sauce
- 1 tablespoon honey
- 1 tablespoon sake
- 2 tablespoon mirin

Method:
1. In a pan over medium heat, combine all of the components for the unagi sauce.
2. Mix until the liquid has browned and is uniformly mixed.
3. Unagi fillets can be cut into short strips.

4.Pour some rice into a cup and finish with unagi sauce for the first serving.

5.Place the unagi pieces on top of the rice and drizzle with additional sauce.

6.Enjoy with a dash of sansho spice powder and nori.

26

JAPANESE UDON NOODLE SOUP

Cooking Time: 25 minutes
Serving Size: 4
Ingredients:
For the Broth
- Salt
- Pepper
- 2 tablespoons mushroom sauce
- ½ teaspoon chili paste
- 2 tablespoons rice vinegar
- ¼ cup soy sauce
- 4 cups vegetable broth
- 1 pinch sugar
- 2 pieces ginger

For Assembling
- ¼ cup cilantro (chopped)
- ½ cup peanuts
- 4 medium green onions
- 1 pound udon noodles

For the Chinese Broccoli
- 2 tablespoons sesame oil

- 1 pound Chinese broccoli
- ½ tablespoon ginger
- 2 cloves garlic
- 1 tablespoon peanut oil

Method:

1. Collect components.

2. Mix the veggie broth or vegan chicken stock with spice, rice vinegar, sugar, mushroom sauce, soy sauce, and chili paste in a small saucepan.

3. To mix, swirl to get to a boil. Turn down the heat and let it boil to a simmer.

4. Enable at least ten minutes for the liquid to boil.

5. For two or three minutes, let that be citrusy and add the minced Chinese kale.

6. Sauté for several moments, till the broccoli is just soft and the color is light green.

7. Cover and set it aside from the fire.

27

HOT POT WITH MISO

Cooking Time: 40 minutes
Serving Size: 4
Ingredients:
- 4 cups water
- Salt, to taste
- 2 pieces of kombu
- 4 Shiitake Mushrooms
- 1 handful Enoki mushrooms
- ½ Napa cabbage
- 1 handful Mizuna greens
- 2 tablespoon white miso paste
- 1 leek, sliced
- 1 dried chili pepper
- 1 tablespoon soy sauce
- 1 turnip, sliced thinly
- 1 small carrot, sliced

Method:

1. Add the water, shiitake mushrooms, leeks, kombu, turnip, carrot, chili pepper, and soy sauce to the pot.

2. For thirty minutes, carry to a light boil.

3. Meanwhile, in a small container, insert the miso and then pour a few cups of water once it becomes a dense sauce texture.

4. This would make the blending of the broth simpler.

5. Switch off the heating after thirty minutes.

6. If required, mix in the miso paste and salts and insert the mizuna, cabbage, and enoki mushroom.

7. Instantly serve.

28

JAPANESE COCO ICHIBANYA-STYLE VEGETABLE CURRY

Cooking Time: 55 minutes
Serving Size: 6
Ingredients:
- 1 box Japanese curry roux mix
- Cooked Japanese rice
- 1 Japanese eggplant
- 8 cherry tomatoes
- 2 tablespoons vegetable oil
- 1 thumb-size fresh ginger
- 2 medium potatoes
- 1 ½ cup green beans
- 1 apple
- 5 cups water
- 1 large carrot
- 1 large onion

Method:
1. Drain in ice water the sliced eggplant and keep for fifteen minutes. Some of the bitterness will be removed from this.
2. Transfer 1 tablespoon oil, grated ginger, and apples to a big saucepan over moderate heat.

3. Insert the onions and roast for three minutes, just until the pieces are transparent and tender.

4. Incorporate liquid and mix. Insert the green beans, carrot, and potatoes and mix.

5. For three minutes, fry on each hand, once crispy and soft.

6. Turn the heat down and shift it to a sheet lined with a clean cloth. Just put aside.

7. Put the lid on again and boil for the remaining two minutes.

8. Serve with fukujinzuke and Japanese fried rice.

29
YAKITORI GRILLED SKEWERS

Cooking Time: 1 hour 5 minutes
Serving Size: 1
Ingredients:
- Spring onions
- Chicken breast

Suggested Additional Items
- Asparagus
- Firm tofu
- Pork belly slices
- Green pepper
- Leek

Sauce
- 1-2 teaspoon katakuriko potato starch
- Shichimi pepper seasoning
- 3 tablespoon soy sauce
- 2 tablespoon sugar
- 1 tablespoon mirin
- 1 tablespoon cooking sake

Method:

1. In a bowl with two tablespoons of sugar, combine the boiling sake, miso, and sesame oil.
2. In a small saucepan, mix a little katakuriko rice flour in water and heat the mixture while boiling it.
3. Start glazing the slicer components with your yakitori sauces using a baking brush.
4. Begin by setting the skewers on the grill in an environment where the heat is high and even.
5. Switch the yakitori often to ensure even cooking, and sprinkle more yakitori sauces onto the meat each time.
6. The meat will be edible once it has turned golden brown.

30

KARAAGE JAPANESE FRIED CHICKEN

Cooking Time: 45 minutes
   Serving Size: 4
   Ingredients:
- ½ teaspoon black pepper
- Lemon wedge
- 1 cup potato starch
- ¼ teaspoon fine sea salt
- 4 skin-on chicken thighs
- Peanut oil
- 1 ½ teaspoons fresh ginger
- 3 tablespoons soy sauce
- 2 teaspoons sugar
- 2 tablespoons dry sake
- 2 teaspoons grated garlic

Method:

   1. Merge the garlic, ginger, rice, sesame oil, and sugar in a small baking dish big enough to hold the meat.

   2. Preheat the oil to 350 degrees Fahrenheit.

   3. Place a sheet pan over a separate cookie sheet as the oil gets hot.

4. Combine rice flour, salt, and peppers in a mixing cup.

5. Fry three or four bits at a time, maintaining a 325°F oil temperature.

6. Double the temperature of the oil to 375 degrees until all of the chicken has been cooked once.

7. Serve with a lemon slice, spinach, and cottage cheese, warm or at ambient temperature.

JAPANESE DINNER AND DESSERTS RECIPES

31

TAMAGO KAKE GOHAN

Cooking Time: 50 minutes
Serving Size: 2
Ingredients:
- 1 scallion, finely chopped
- Sesame seeds, for sprinkling
- Extra-virgin olive oil
- 2 eggs
- Splashes of tamari
- 3 cups cooked brown rice

Method:

1. Squeeze out two cups of fried brown rice.

2. Put 1 egg per cup alongside splatters of tamari when the rice is boiling, and mix rapidly so that the egg heats softly while the rice covers, giving the rice a creamy texture.

3. Cover each cup with spring onions, pumpkin seeds, and the extra toppings you want. Serve on the surface with miso for flavor.

32

LIGHTLY FRIED JAPANESE VEGETABLES

Cooking Time: 20 minutes
Serving Size: 2
Ingredients:
- Sea salt
- Toasted sesame seeds
- ¼ white cabbage, julienned
- 2 teaspoons mirin
- Sesame oil
- 1 tablespoon rice wine vinegar
- 1 tablespoon tamari
- 2 carrots, julienned
- 1 small red bell pepper
- 1 small white onion
- 4 spring onions, chopped
- 1 zucchini, thinly sliced

Method:
1. Over a high flame, warm up a big wok.
2. Insert the sesame oil and transfer the veggies until it is close to the combustion mark.

3. Let them stay in a wok until half of the wok is dark on one edge.

4. Mix the tamari, vinegar, and mirin of rice wine.

5. When stirring, spray the combination over the veggies to offer them some humidity.

6. To ensure they are always crisp, cook the veggies for two minutes.

7. If required, sprinkle them with kosher salt, put them on serving plates, and marinade them with toasted pine nuts.

33

VEGETABLE GYOZA

Cooking Time: 2 hours
  Serving Size: 80
  Ingredients:
For Gyoza Filling
- 1 clove garlic
- 2 tablespoon potato starch
- 2 green onions
- 1 knob ginger
- 12 oz. extra firm tofu
- 5 oz. king oyster mushrooms
- 2 oz. carrot
- 3 oz. onion
- 2 oz. shiitake mushrooms
- 5 oz. cabbage
- 1 teaspoon kosher salt
- 3.5 oz. red cabbage

For Dipping Sauce
- 1/8 teaspoon la-yu
- 1 tablespoon soy sauce
- 1 tablespoon rice vinegar

For Gyoza Filling Seasonings
- 1 teaspoon kosher salt
- ⅛ teaspoon white pepper powder
- 1 tablespoon miso
- 2 teaspoon sesame oil
- 2 tablespoon soy sauce

For Frying Gyoza
- ¼ cup water
- 1 teaspoon sesame oil (roasted)
- 1 tablespoon oil

For Gyoza
- Water
- 80 Gyoza wrappers

Method:

1. Collect all the components. Place a washcloth over the tofu and put it on a tray.

2. Place another layer on top of the tofu, then, with a large weight or two, force the tofu hard for about one hour.

3. Put two tablespoons of soy sauce, two teaspoons of sesame oil, one tablespoon of miso, and ⅛ teaspoon of white pepper into a small pan.

4. Add the two types of mushroom, carrots, onion, and spring onions, into a big cup.

5. Then continue cooking, and add garlic, which is minced.

6. In the pan, add the tofu blocks and the Gyoza Filled Spice combination and blend it.

7. Over medium pressure, steam the oil in a pan non-stick deep fryer. When it is hot in the skillet, put the Gyoza.

8. Cook for about three minutes before the Gyoza tops turn light golden. To the bowl, add ¼ cup of hot water.

9. Bring the sauce components together for the dipping sauce. Serve hot.

34

TOFU KATSU WITH SPICY SWEET-SOUR SAUCE

Cooking Time: 15 minutes
Serving Size: 24
Ingredients:
- Sunflower or canola oil
- Sweet chili sauce, to serve
- ½ cup Aquafaba
- ½-1 cup breadcrumbs
- 200 grams firm tofu
- 2 tablespoon plain flour
- Soy sauce

Method:
1. First, to eliminate the extra humidity and digest flavors faster, we have to 'push' the tofu.
2. Shift it to a fresh one until the paper towel gets wet. Repeat till the hand towel remains almost clean.
3. When the tofu is pounded, split the cube in half and finish with two layers that are fifty percent thinner.
4. Pour ample soy sauce so that the tofu is at least half immersed.

5.Left it for thirty minutes to marinate, then turn over the tofu bits and keep for the next 30 minutes in soy sauce.

6.To create an even coverage on both sides, ensure you push each square's surface into the powder and cornflour well.

7.Push few more bits of tofu into the butter.

35

JAPANESE VEGETABLE STEW WITH MISO BROTH

Cooking Time: 50 minutes
Serving Size: 4
Ingredients:
- 2 teaspoon soy sauce
- 2 cups dashi (stock)
- 2 tablespoon sake
- 2 tablespoon miso
- 375 grams sweet potato
- 200 grams Napa cabbage
- 300 grams carrots
- 1 tablespoon vegetable oil
- 200 grams leeks
- 600 grams kabocha squash
- 4 shiitake mushrooms

Method:
1. Start preparing the dashi 8-24 hours until you cook.

2. Keep it to use in the soup when you use entire shiitake mushrooms in the dashi.

3. Place the sweet potato in a container large enough to accommodate the squash as well.

4.Break the squash into bits the size of a bite. Place the squash along with the sweet potato in a dish.

5.Set the whites portion of the napa apart from the greenery portion.

6.Over medium pressure, heat the liquid. Insert any leeks.

7.Heat until tender, constantly stirring, for five minutes.

8.Insert the sake as well as cook, sealed, for approximately two minutes.

9.Squash and sweet potato are added. Swirl.

10.Transfer the napa cabbage and mushroom to the top part.

11.Cover and simmer for five minutes.

12.Stir in the soy sauce and turn the heat down to a low level.

36

15 MINUTE SPICY UDON

Cooking Time: 15 minutes
Serving Size: 2
Ingredients:
Stir Fry
- 3 cups baby spinach
- 14 oz. soft udon noodles
- 1 medium carrot
- 1 cup green onion
- ½ medium onion
- 1 tablespoon vegetable oil

Sauce
- 2 cloves garlic
- 1 teaspoon sesame oil
- 2 tablespoon brown sugar
- 1 tablespoon fresh ginger
- ¼ cup soy sauce
- 2 teaspoon rice wine vinegar
- 2 teaspoon Sambal Oelek

For Garnish
- Additional green onion

5. Shake off any particles of salts that remain.

6. In a tiny, hard bottom frying pan, put the Shaoxing wine, mirin, sugar, sake, ginger, sesame oil, and miso paste on low.

7. Cook for thirty minutes in the well-heated oven until golden and soft.

8. Spray with sesame oil and eat warm with coconut rice and daikon.

NO-BAKE CRÈME CARAMEL

Cooking Time: 50 minutes
Serving Size: 8
Ingredients:
Caramel Sauce
- 2 tablespoon water
- 2 tablespoon boiling water
- ⅔ cup sugar

Custard
- ½ cup heavy cream
- 2 teaspoon pure vanilla extract
- 80g sugar
- 1¾ cups whole milk
- ¼ cup water
- 4 large egg yolks
- 4 sheets gelatin powder

Method:
1. Assemble all of the necessary ingredients.
2. In a small saucepan, mix the water and sugar.
3. Gently stir and rotate the pan again to evenly disperse the solution.

4. Remove the pan from the heat and place it on a cool, damp towel before adding boiling water.
5. Heat the ramekins in warm water for a few seconds.
6. Allocate the caramel equally among the eight ramekins while it is still sweet.
7. Remove the pan from the fire and set it aside.
8. Mix the egg whites and sugar in a big bowl and mix until light and fluffy.
9. Heat dairy in a small saucepan until it becomes hot to the touch.
10. Slowly drizzle in the wet milk.
11. Re-insert the solution into the frying pan.
12. Cook, moving continuously, over medium-low pressure.
13. Fill the ramekins halfway with the custard.

39
VEGETABLE YAKISOBA

Cooking Time: 40 minutes
Serving Size: 10
Ingredients:
- 16 oz. yakisoba noodles
- 3 tablespoon oil
- ¼ small cabbage
- 1 large onion
- ½ lb. broccoli
- 2 large carrots
- 1 large sweet bell pepper

Yakisoba Sauce
- 2 tablespoon ketchup
- 4 tablespoon Worcestershire sauce
- 2 tablespoon soy sauce
- 2 tablespoon oyster sauce
- 2 tablespoon sugar

Method:
1. Mix all yakisoba liquid ingredients in a large bowl and set aside.
2. Heat a small amount of oil in a skillet over high heat.

3. Return all of the veggies to the same pan. Separate the noodles as directed on the box. Toss in the noodles in the skillet.

4. Toss all together after pouring the sauce over the components.

5. Reduce the heat to medium-low and cook for five minutes.

6. Take it off the heat and enjoy it!

40

SZECHUAN EGGPLANT

Cooking Time: 45 minutes
Serving Size: 4
Ingredients:
- 2 teaspoons ginger
- 10 dried red chilies
- 4 tablespoons peanut oil
- 4 cloves garlic
- 2 teaspoons salt
- 2 tablespoons cornstarch
- 1½ lbs. Japanese Eggplant

Szechuan Sauce
- 3 tablespoons sugar
- ½ teaspoon five-spice
- 1 tablespoon rice vinegar
- 1 tablespoon cooking wine
- 1 teaspoon Szechuan peppercorns
- 1 tablespoon garlic chili paste
- 1 tablespoon sesame oil
- ¼ cup soy sauce

Method:

1. Cut the eggplant into ½ inch slices.
2. Place in a large mixing bowl with two teaspoons salts and fill with water.
3. Meanwhile, finely cut the ginger and garlic.
4. In a dry pan, toast the Szechuan peppers.
5. In a small cup, whisk together these and the leftover marinade.
6. Combine the eggplant and corn starch in a mixing bowl.
7. Add one tablespoon of further oil to the skillet and cook the ginger and garlic for two minutes over low heat, stirring constantly.
8. Serve in a casserole plate with shallots on top.

41

JAPANESE FRUIT SANDWICH

Cooking Time: 10 minutes
Serving Size: 4
Ingredients:
- ¼ teaspoon vanilla extract
- 8 slices Japanese sandwich bread
- ½ pint heavy cream
- 3½ tablespoons milk
- 1 mango
- 14 strawberries
- 1 kiwi fruit

Method:

1. Cut the kiwifruit into ¾-inch thick circles after peeling and slicing it.

2. Remove the peel from the mango, remove the tapered ends, and cut it into ¾-inch wide batons.

3. Strawberry tops can be removed. If they are too big, cut them in half.

4. In a cold pan, whisk together the heavy cream, condensed milk, and vanilla essence until strong peaks emerge.

5. Fruit should be put on top of the whipped cream.

6. Take the crusts from the four remaining bits of toast and cover the sandwiches.

7. Cut them in half or quarters until you are about to eat them.

42

STRAWBERRY MOCHI

Cooking Time: 25 minutes
　Serving Size: 6
Ingredients:
- 180g sweet white bean paste
- 6 medium-sized strawberry
- 200ml water
- Katakuriko potato starch
- 30g sugar
- 180g Shiratamako

Method:
1. Remove the stems from the berries and wash them.
2. In a big heatproof bowl, combine Shiratamako and sugar, then add more water.
3. Reheat for another minute after stirring well with a dough scraper.
4. Load the mochi cup onto the starch and sprinkle ample Karakuriko on the rolling pad.
5. Split the mochi into five sections and roll each one out flat to a diameter of around 10 cm.

6.Position the strawberry covered in white bean paste on the stretched-out mochi.

7.Using well-dusted paws, collect the surface of the mochi covering and wrap the berries in it.

8.Toss in the leftover mochi and berries and continue the cycle.

MOST FAMOUS JAPANESE DISHES

43

JAPANESE MITARASHI DANGO

Cooking Time: 15 minutes
Serving Size: 2
Ingredients:
- 4 tablespoon filtered water
- ½ cup sweet rice flour (mochiko)

Sauce
- 2 teaspoon mirin
- 1 teaspoon arrowroot starch
- 1 tablespoon soy sauce
- 1 tablespoon coconut sugar
- 3 tablespoon filtered water

Other
- Wood skewers
- Toasted nori sheet

Method:

1. Over moderate flame, ready a pot of boiling water, and bring it to a boil when cooking your Dango flour.

2. Mix the water and sweet rice flour in a measuring dish.

3. Proceed with a spoon and mix to blend, then begin using your hands to work the flour.

4. Break into 6 bits and shape into little balls until you have a functional dough.

5. Drop softly into the pot while the water boils and steam for about five minutes, and until the Dango is floating and is baked all the time through.

6. First, mix gluten-free soy sauce, coconut sugar, water, and mirin in a shallow skillet over medium heat.

7. Stir to mix, add the slurry of arrowroot flour and begin stirring until the mixture thickens.

8. Turn off the heat until the sauce thickens, then put it aside.

9. Drain the Dango again, though, and skewer three bits with each piece.

10. Glaze to the palate of your sweet soy glaze and eat!

44

CREAMY MISO PASTA WITH TOFU AND ASPARAGUS

Cooking Time: 20 minutes
Serving Size: 2
Ingredients:
For Pasta
- ¼ teaspoon kosher
- Freshly ground black pepper
- 1 firm fried tofu
- 1 tablespoon olive oil
- 4 oz. asparagus

For Cooking Spaghetti
- 2 teaspoon miso
- 1 teaspoon soy sauce
- Soy milk sauce
- ½ cup unsweetened soy milk
- 7 oz. spaghetti
- 1 ½ tablespoon sea salt

Method:
1. Collect all the components.
2. Mix a half cup of soy milk, two teaspoons of miso, and one teaspoon of soy sauce in a mixing cup and blend it.

3. Approximately twice the sum of these components if you want to turn it into "soup noodles."

4. With a clean cloth, cover the tofu and extract any humidity. Split into small pieces of tofu.

5. Cut off the asparagus edges and cut them into small slices horizontally.

6. Begin to boil four quarters of water in a big saucepan. Put one and a half tablespoon of salt and pasta until boiling.

7. To the bowl, transfer the soy flour mixture and reduce the heat to a moderate flame.

8. For separate pots, serve the spaghetti.

45

WAGAMAMA WOK-FRIED GREENS

Cooking Time: 20 minutes
Serving Size: 2
Ingredients:
For the Sauce
- 1 tablespoon sesame oil
- Ground black pepper
- 1 teaspoon sugar
- 2 tablespoons soy sauce

For the Greens
- 150g tender stem broccoli
- 200g pak choi
- 2 garlic cloves
- 2 tablespoons oil

Method:

1. In a small mixing bowl, combine all of the sauce components.

2. In a slow cooker or cooking pan, add the oil.

3. Fry the garlic for about thirty seconds on medium heat until aromatic and golden brown – be careful not to damage it!

4. Combine the broccoli, bok choy, and liquid in a large mixing bowl.

5. Heat, frequently stirring, for around five minutes, or until veggies are cooked to your taste.

6. Taste, and if possible, add more soy sauce.

46

JAPANESE SOBA NOODLES

Cooking Time: 20 minutes
Serving Size: 6
Ingredients:
- ½ cup green onions minced
- 3 tablespoons sesame seeds
- 1 tablespoon canola oil
- 2 cups green onions
- 10 ounces Soba Buckwheat Noodles
- ¼ teaspoon ground black pepper
- 1 tablespoon sugar
- 1/3 cup Double Fermented Soy Sauce
- 3 tablespoons toasted sesame oil
- 2 tablespoons rice vinegar

Method:

1. Carry a big pot of water on the stove and make soup the soba pasta for five minutes or even just until soft, occasionally mixing so the pasta does not tangle.

2. Wash in a colander and pat dry under ice water, dumping to erase the starch.

3. When the pasta is frying, sweep the sesame oil, soy sauce,

sugar rice vinegar, and black pepper together in such a small dish. And put aside.

4. Over medium flame, heat a large skillet.

5. Insert the canola oil and flame the sliced spring onions until they glitter.

6. Heat for fifteen seconds or until aromatic, mixing.

7. Insert the sesame and soy mixture and reheat for thirty seconds.

8. Put the pasta and toss till the pasta is warmed through.

9. Insert the leftover minced spring onions and a quarter of the seeds.

10. Garnish with the residual seeds and eat at low temperatures or hotter.

47

SOY-GLAZED EGGPLANT DONBURI

Cooking Time: 20 minutes
Serving Size: 2
Ingredients:
- 4 tablespoon neutral-flavored oil
- ½ teaspoon white sesame seeds
- 1 knob ginger
- 2 tablespoon potato starch
- 10 shiso leaves
- 7 oz. Japanese eggplant

Seasonings
- 2 tablespoon soy sauce
- 4 tablespoon mirin

Method:
1. Collect all the components.
2. Round the eggplant into ¼-inch pieces and insert iodine.
3. Put aside for fifteen minutes and put a hand towel to clean off the humidity.
4. Wash the shiso leaf and use a hand towel to clear. Dispose of the ends.

5. Heat 2 tablespoons of oil over medium-high heat in a cooking pot.

6. Add the eggplant pieces to a thin layer when the pan is heated.

7. Cook till it is nicely browned on the back end, around three minutes.

8. Do not hit the eggplants before then to obtain a good sear.

9. Whenever the lowest surface is perfectly fried, sprinkle on top of the remaining oil (2 tablespoons) and turn the eggplant slices for around 3-4 minutes to fry the other half.

10. Take it down to a boil and spill the sauce a couple of times over the eggplant.

11. Spray with seeds and decorate with shiso leaves. Instantly serve.

48

JAPANESE MUSHROOM STIR-FRY

Cooking Time: 10 minutes
Serving Size: 2
Ingredients:
- 2 tablespoon fermented soybeans
- 8 shiitake mushrooms
- 1 small eggplant
- 1 clove garlic
- 2 tablespoon vegetable oil
- 1 x 2cm piece of ginger

Sauce
- 1 tablespoon mirin
- 1 tablespoon miso paste
- 1 tablespoon soy sauce
- ½ teaspoon sesame oil
- 2 teaspoon sugar

Method:
1. Whisk together all of the sauce components.
2. In a warm skillet, add oil and the garlic and ginger, and fry until translucent.
3. Toss the veggies in the skillet with the oil.

4. Toss in the sliced eggplant and mushrooms for two minutes, just until the eggplant softens.

5. Toss in the liquid, bring to the boil, and toss once more.

6. Turn off the heat after adding the soybeans and tossing them through.

7. Serve hot with beans.

JAPANESE SHIITAKE AND VEGETABLE RICE

Cooking Time: 2 hours 30 minutes
Serving Size: 6
Ingredients:
- 2 scallions, thinly sliced
- ¼ cup frozen peas
- 6 ounces shiitake mushrooms
- ½ cup diced carrot
- 1 ½ cups short-grain brown rice
- 2 tablespoons reduced-sodium tamari
- Pinch of salt
- 2 tablespoons mirin
- 2 ½ cups Dashi Stock

Method:
1. In a medium skillet, place the rice and bring water to fill 2 inches.
2. To release the ground starch, squirt with your fingertips.
3. Drain boiling liquid off and repeat it two to three times, just until the liquid is almost clean.
4. In a sieve, spill the rice and leave to drain for five minutes.

5. Move the sieve a couple of times, then bring the rice back to the plate.

6. Over moderate flame, take the solution to a lively boil, stirring regularly.

7. Take it out of the flame and let it stay for ten minutes.

8. Over the tip, sprinkle the peas instead of filler the rice and blend with the lentils.

9. Wrap and then let stand for about ten minutes, till the peas are cooled. Before eating, whisk in the spring onion greens.

50

SPICY TOFU BENTO BOWL

Cooking Time: 30 minutes
Serving Size: 6
Ingredients:
- 2 tablespoon sesame seeds
- 2-3 scallions, sliced thinly
- 1 teaspoon red chili flakes
- 1 lb. broccolini, about 12 stalks
- 2 garlic cloves, finely minced
- 2 teaspoon ginger, minced
- 1 tablespoon white miso paste
- 1 tablespoon brown sugar
- 1 cup dry brown or white rice
- 3 tablespoon soy sauce
- 2 tablespoon rice vinegar
- 3 tablespoon sesame oil
- 6 Portobello mushrooms

Method:
1. In a cup, combine the sesame oil, chili-garlic sauce, and soy sauce.

2. Over medium-high heat, warm a pan. Soak the tofu in a soy sauce combination; boil for ten minutes, or until golden brown.

3. Transfer the leftover chili combination to the spring onions, cream, and lime juice. Toss on the tofu.

4. In a cup, combine the soy sauce, lime juice, spice, and chili-garlic sauce.

5. Add rice in bowls for dining. Top of the Greens.

6. Trim carrot stripes with a cheese grater over the end.

7. Place the tofu, celery, and carrot on top. Slather with sesame seeds; eat with a combination of soya sauce.

51
YASAI ITAME

Cooking Time: 30 minutes
Serving Size: 4
Ingredients:
- 1 tablespoon neutral-flavored oil
- 3.5 oz. bean sprouts
- 1 clove garlic
- 1 knob ginger
- 6.5 oz. thinly sliced pork
- ¼ cabbage
- ½ carrot
- ¼ onion
- 10 snow peas

For Pork Marinade
- 1 teaspoon sake
- 1 teaspoon soy sauce

For Seasonings
- Freshly ground black pepper
- 2 teaspoon sesame oil
- 1 teaspoon soy sauce
- ½ teaspoon kosher salt

- 1 teaspoon oyster sauce

Method:

1. Assemble all the components.
2. If needed, cut meat into tiny chunks and sauté the beef in a shallow saucepan with one teaspoon of soy sauce and one teaspoon of sake.
3. Strip the snow peas from the loops and cut the onions into small strips.
4. Heat 2 tablespoons of olive oil over moderate heat in a large deep fryer or skillet.
5. Insert the onion and cook till almost soft, then add the carrots and mix.
6. Insert the broccoli and green beans as the carrot is growing soft.
7. Keep stirring the components and mix.
8. Insert one tablespoon of oyster sauce and one teaspoon of soya sauce.
9. Insert the cinnamon, chili flakes, freshly roasted, and drizzle with two teaspoons of sesame oil.

52

LIGHTLY FRIED JAPANESE VEGETABLES

Cooking Time: 20 minutes
Serving Size: 2
Ingredients:
- Sea salt
- Toasted sesame seeds
- ¼ white cabbage, julienned
- 2 teaspoons mirin
- Sesame oil
- 1 tablespoon rice wine vinegar
- 1 tablespoon tamari
- 2 carrots, julienned
- 1 small red bell pepper
- 1 small white onion
- 4 spring onions, chopped
- 1 zucchini, thinly sliced

Method:
8. Over a high flame, warm up a big wok.
9. Insert the sesame oil and transfer the veggies until it is close to the combustion mark.

10. Let them stay in a wok until half of the wok is dark on one edge.

11. Mix the tamari, vinegar, and mirin of rice wine.

12. When stirring, spray the combination over the veggies to offer them some humidity.

13. To ensure they are always crisp, cook the veggies for two minutes.

53

HEARTY VEGETABLE MISO SOUP

Cooking Time: 30 minutes
Serving Size: 4
Ingredients:
- 2 potatoes
- 1-2 carrots (peeled)
- 1 onion
- 5-6 mushrooms
- 2 tablespoon peanut oil
- 4 tablespoon miso paste
- 4 cups water

Method:
1. Split herbs, no bigger than ¾-inch, into small bites.
2. Sauté the vegetables in a broth sauté pan in heated oil till they become transparent; then insert the other veggies and sauté for another three minutes.
3. Add the water and cook till all veggies are tender; minimize heat to medium and insert miso paste to boil.
4. Bring to a boil and add diced leeks or cut spring onions to flavor.

54

KURIGOHAN (CHESTNUT RICE)

Cooking Time: 45 minutes
Serving Size: 6
Ingredients:
- 1 tablespoon soy sauce
- Black sesame seeds
- 1 tablespoon sake
- 1 tablespoon mirin
- 400g Japanese short-grain rice
- 600 ml water
- 400g jarred Kuri chestnuts
- 50g sweet mochi rice

Method:
1. Wash and drain the rice immediately.
2. In a big mixing bowl, combine all rice and rinse with ice water until the water flows clean.
3. In a big pan, mix the rice, liquid, sake, miso, and sesame oil.
4. Bring to a boil, then shield and decrease to low heat for around 20 minutes, just until the rice consumes the water.
5. Remove the rice from the heat source.

6. The chestnuts are then added and covered with a cap for ten minutes to heat up.

7. Serve in bowls of black sesame seeds on top and eat.

55

JAPANESE STIR-FRIED NOODLES WITH VEGGIES

Cooking Time: 30 minutes
   Serving Size: 3
Ingredients:
- 2 teaspoon soy sauce
- 2 teaspoon sugar
- 4 teaspoon oyster sauce
- 4 teaspoon ketchup
- ½ onion
- 1 carrot
- 4-6 tablespoon yakisoba sauce
- 4 tablespoon Worcestershire sauce
- 3 shiitake mushrooms
- Freshly ground black pepper
- 3 servings of yakisoba noodles
- 2 green onions
- ¾ lb. sliced pork belly
- 2 tablespoon neutral-flavored oil
- 4 cabbage leaves

Method:
1. Gather all of the necessary ingredients.

2. To make the Yakisoba paste, whisk together all of the components.

3. Break the onion into slices, the carrot into diced pieces, and the shiitake mushrooms into chunks.

4. Heat the oil in a pan or skillet over moderate flame.

5. Cook the vegetables until it is wilted in the center.

6. Cook for 1-2 minutes after adding the onion and carrots.

7. Cook till the cabbage is almost soft.

8. Heat for 1 minute after adding the spring onions and butternut squash.

9. Season with smoked paprika, fresh roasted.

10. Add the Yakisoba Sauce and change the quantity depending on the rest of the ingredients. Serve right away.

56

HIBACHI VEGETABLES

Cooking Time: 20 minutes
Serving Size: 4
Ingredients:
- ½ teaspoon sesame seeds
- Salt and pepper to taste
- 1 tablespoon soy sauce
- 2 tablespoons teriyaki sauce
- 2 cups broccoli florets
- 8 oz. mushrooms
- 2 tablespoons butter
- 1 zucchini
- 1 cup carrots
- ½ tablespoon garlic
- ½ sweet onion
- 1 tablespoon oil

Method:

1. Melt butter in a skillet over medium-high heat, then add the oil and sauté tomatoes and ginger for two minutes, until it's tender.

2. Zucchini, cabbage, lettuce, and mushrooms are all good additions.

3. Dress with salt and pepper to taste after adding the sesame oil and teriyaki sauce.

4. Cook for ten minutes, or until the vegetables are tender.

5. Serve immediately with toasted pine nuts scattered on top.

JAPANESE RAMEN AND SUSHI RECIPES

57

VEGETARIAN RAMEN

Cooking Time: 1 hour
Serving Size: 4
Ingredients:
- 4 baby bok choy
- 4 5-oz. packages ramen noodles
- 3 tablespoon unsalted butter
- 1 tablespoon soy sauce
- 4 garlic cloves
- 8 dried shiitake mushrooms
- 1 piece dried kombu
- ¼ cup vegetable oil
- 1 2" piece ginger
- 2 tablespoon tomato paste
- 1 tablespoon black sesame seeds
- Kosher salt
- 4 scallions
- 1 tablespoon. gochugaru

Method:
1. Cook the garlic and ¼ cup of the oil in a medium saucepan

over medium heat, frequently whisking, until the garlic is translucent, around four minutes.

2. Heat the remaining two tablespoons of oil to moderate in the preserved pot.

3. Insert the tomato sauce and simmer for about two minutes, stirring regularly, before it appears to adhere to the sides of the pan and blackens gradually.

4. Insert the Kombu and mushroom, then whisk in five cups of cold water.

5. Move the solids to a mixer using a rubber spatula.

6. To mix, add a spoonful or two of liquid and purée until creamy.

7. Add oil a slice at a time, until introducing more, whisking to mix with each addition.

8. In the meantime, put it to a boil with a big pot of water. Insert bok choy and cook for about two minutes until it is greenish and soft.

58
INSTANT POT RAMEN RECIPE

Cooking Time: 25 minutes
Serving Size: 6
Ingredients:
- Black and white sesame
- Chili oil
- 2 tablespoons soy sauce
- 4 stalks scallion
- 3 packages of ramen noodles
- 8 oz. bok choy
- 1 lb. chicken tenders
- 2 cups water
- 4 eggs
- Salt
- 1 ½ tablespoon vegetable oil
- 4 cups chicken broth
- Ground black pepper

Method:
1. On all sides of the meat, sprinkle with salt and ground black pepper.
2. Switch the Instant Pot to Sauté stage.

3. Sear the poultry in an oven until both sides are golden brown.

4. Add chicken stock, water, and the green onions white bits.

5. Bring to a simmer and switch the pressure cooker to "Automatic" for ten minutes.

6. Make the ramen eggs in the meantime.

7. Switch the Instant Pot to Fast Release as it buzzes.

8. Then insert the bok choy and sesame oil. Toss the ramen about a little.

9. Cover the pot and switch off the Sauté mode.

10. The ramen noodles can be divided into four cups.

11. Serve the ramen right away.

59

TONKATSU RAMEN SOUP

Cooking Time: 15 minutes
Serving Size: 2
Ingredients:
- 1 green onion
- 1 teaspoon of sesame oil
- Water
- 1½ tablespoon of dashi stock
- 2 tablespoon of usukuchi soy sauce
- 1½ tablespoon of Weipa

Method:
1. Heat all of the condiments together in an oven.
2. Vegetable buds or green onion heads may be added.
3. Include an instant ramen bar.
4. Bring to a boil, and insert sesame oil.
5. Add one tablespoon each of condiments and sesame oil.
6. Heat for five minutes and serve right away.

60

CHICKEN RAMEN

Cooking Time: 1 hour
Serving Size: 2
Ingredients:
- 2 (3 oz.) packs ramen noodles
- Fresh jalapeño slices
- 2 large eggs
- ½ cup scallions
- 2 chicken breasts
- 1 oz. shitake mushrooms
- 1–2 teaspoon sea salt, to taste
- Kosher salt
- 2 tablespoon mirin
- 4 cups rich chicken stock
- Black pepper
- 3 teaspoon fresh garlic
- 3 tablespoon soy sauce
- 2 teaspoon sesame oil
- 2 teaspoon fresh ginger
- 1 tablespoon unsalted butter

Method:

1. Preheat oven to 375 degrees Fahrenheit.
2. Dress the chicken with salt and pepper.
3. In a big oven-safe pan, heat the oil over medium-high heat.
4. Cook the chicken with the skin cut side.
5. Roast for twenty minutes in the oven with the pan.
6. In a big pot, add the oil over a moderate flame until it shimmers.
7. Get the stocks to a boil, covered, before adding the dried mushrooms.
8. To make the soft-boiled whites, first cook the eggs in salted water.
9. Slice the green onion and jalapeno in the meantime.
10. Then use a sharp knife, cut the chicken into thin slices.
11. Cook for three minutes, just until the noodles are tender, then split into two big bowls.
12. Mix the cut chicken and ramen broth in a large mixing bowl.
13. Small green onion, jalapeno, and a soft boiled egg go on edge. Serve right away.

61

SAVORY MUSHROOM AND VEGETABLE RAMEN SOUP

Cooking Time: 40 minutes
Serving Size: 2
Ingredients:
- Salt, to taste
- Red chili flakes (optional)
- Juice from 1 lime
- Olive oil
- 6 ounces ramen noodles
- 2 cloves of garlic, diced
- 1 small shallot, diced
- 4 cups mushroom broth
- 1 cup baby kale
- ¼ cup grated rainbow carrots
- 1 cup broccoli
- ½ cup beech mushrooms
- 1 cup shiitake mushrooms

Method:

1. Heat the broccoli, then preheat the pan on the stove over hot water and insert some olive oil.

2. Transfer to the pot two minced garlic cloves and a tiny shal-

lot, let them boil once transparent and afterward insert diced mushrooms.

3. Heat the mushrooms, cloves, and shallot for several minutes, then insert a tamari dash and little kale sauces and simmer until the kale begins to ripen.

4. Transfer the soup and pasta to a container with kale, mushrooms, and broccoli whenever the pasta is heated.

5. On edge, grind some rainbow vegetables, red chili powder, a combination of natural seaweed particles, a sprinkle of pepper, and one lemon juice.

62

SPICY VEGETARIAN RAMEN

Cooking Time: 30 minutes
Serving Size: 2
Ingredients:
- 1 tablespoon sesame seeds
- 1 tablespoon red chili flakes
- ¼ cup avocado oil
- 3 cloves garlic
- 5 ounces ramen noodles
- Fried garlic and chili oil
- 2 tablespoon Sriracha
- 2 tablespoon low-sodium soy sauce
- 4 cups vegetable broth
- 2 tablespoon tomato paste
- 2 tablespoon light sesame oil
- 3 cloves garlic
- 4 scallions
- ¾-1 cup porcini mushrooms

Method:
1. Place the roasted garlic in the sesame oil first. Over moderate temperature, heat ¼ cup of oil in a large pan.

2. Add finely chopped cloves and pan-fry when heated, constantly stirring, until the garlic just begins to turn translucent, approximately three minutes.

3. Fry until fragrant, two minutes, approximately.

4. Add the broth, tomato sauce, soy sauce, and Sriracha.

5. Boil, uncovered, for ten minutes over moderate flame.

6. Prepare your selection of toppings, although the broth simmers.

7. Offer a little flavor to the soup and, as needed, more season.

8. Cook the pasta immediately in the boiling broth for a smoother ramen soup for approximately 3-4 minutes to tender, or before soft.

9. Cover instant noodles and soup with a rain of spice oil and add all your favorite condiments.

63
RICH AND CREAMY TONKOTSU RAMEN BROTH RECIPE

Cooking Time: 12 to 18 hours
Serving Size: 6 to 8
Ingredients:
- 6 ounces whole mushrooms
- 1 pound slab pork fatback
- 2 whole leeks
- 12 garlic cloves
- One 3-inch knob ginger
- 2 dozen scallions
- 2 tablespoons vegetable oil
- 1 large onion, skin on
- 2 pounds chicken backs and carcasses
- 3 pounds pig trotters

Method:
1. Fill a big stockpot halfway with cold water and add the pork and chicken bones.
2. Bring a pot of water to a boil over medium temperature.
3. Combine the onions, cloves, and ginger in a large mixing bowl.
4. Return the roasted tomatoes, leeks, spring onion whites,

mushrooms, and meat fatback to the oven. Fill the container with cold water.

5. Heat over medium heat until the broth is decreased to around three quarts.

6. Cooked pork fatback should be finely chopped and whisked into the finished broth.

7. Dress broth with toppings of your choice before serving.

64

NIGIRIZUSHI

Cooking Time: 30 minutes
   Serving Size: 1
   Ingredients:
   •Nori; as needed
   •Nikiri sauce
   •Wasabi; as needed
   •Sushi rice
   Method:

1. Break the nori into pieces for nigirizushi that include a string of nori to tie the sushi intact.

2. Add a tiny knob of wasabi to the grain for nigirizushi that needs it between both the rice and the coating.

3. Place the topping of your choice on top of the rice noodles.

4. If nori is being used, coil one of the nori band ends tightly around the nigiri sushi coating, ensuring that it adheres to the rice and filling.

5. Use a small volume of spray, wet the other nori bands' end, and loop it around the topping, overlapping the other nori side.

6. The nori ends to hold together as a result of the warm water. Serve right away.

65

SUSHI RICE

Cooking Time: 25 minutes
Serving Size: 15
Ingredients:
- ¼ cup white sugar
- 1 teaspoon salt
- ½ cup rice vinegar
- 1 tablespoon vegetable oil
- 3 cups water
- 2 cups white rice

Method:

1. In a ramekin or strainer, wash the grain until the water flows clean.
2. In a small saucepan, mix the ingredients with the water.
3. Bring to the boil, then decrease to medium heat and simmer for 20 minutes, covered.
4. Water should be consumed, and the rice should be soft.
5. Allow cooling before you can handle it.
6. Mix the rice wine vinegar, oil, butter, and salt in a shallow saucepan.

7.Cook until the sugar has dissolved over medium-high heat.
8.Allow cooling before stirring into the boiled rice.
9.Continue to stir the rice as it condenses, and it may dry out.

66

CHAWANMUSHI

Cooking Time: 30 minutes
Serving Size: 4
Ingredients:
- Pinch of salt
- Tsuyu
- 1 teaspoon soy sauce
- 1 teaspoon sugar
- 3 eggs
- 8 slices kamaboko steamed fish cake
- 1 teaspoon cooking sake
- 4 large cooked prawns
- 4 shiitake mushrooms
- 240ml dashi stock

Method:

1. Begin by gently whisking the eggs in a mixing cup, making sure they do not froth up.

2. Combine the dashi storage, sesame oil, boiling sake, sugar, and salt in a separate dish.

3. To get a decent blend, add this mixture to the eggs when stirring constantly.

4.Pour the water from the shiitake mushrooms, strip the roots, and cut in half.

5.A shallow bowl or cup for each places two cut shiitake pieces, one big prawn, and double slices of kamaboko.

6.Filled the cups up to the brim with the beaten egg.

67

KITSUNE UDON

Cooking Time: 20 minutes
Serving Size: 2
Ingredients:
For Soup Broth
- 1 tablespoon usukuchi soy sauce
- ½ teaspoon kosher salt
- 1 tablespoon mirin
- 1 teaspoon sugar
- 2 ¼ cups dashi

For Kitsune Udon
- 4 slices narutomaki
- Shichimi Togarashi
- 4 inari age
- 1 green onion
- 2 servings of udon noodles

For Homemade Dashi
- 1 kombu
- 1 ½ cups katsuobushi
- 2 ½ cups water

Method:

1. In a measurement cup, combine the Kombu and 2 ½ cup water for at least thirty minutes.

2. Rinse for three hours or upwards to half a day if you have the room.

3. In a saucepan, combine the Kombu and the water.

4. Over moderate pressure, slowly bring to a simmer.

5. Reduce the heat to low and allow the dashi to simmer for fifteen seconds before turning off the heat.

6. Take the dashi, miso, one teaspoon salt, sesame oil, and sugar to a boil in a saucepan.

7. For the udon noodles, bring a big pot of water to the stove.

8. In a pot of boiling water, steam the dried udon noodles for ten minutes.

9. In serving pots, combine udon noodles and spicy broth.

68

CUTLET RICE BOWL KATSUDON

Cooking Time: 40 minutes
Serving Size: 2
Ingredients:
- Chopped green onion
- 2 bowls of cooked rice

For The Katsu
- 1 tablespoon milk
- 100g panko breadcrumbs
- 4 tablespoon plain flour
- 1 large egg
- Pinch of salt and pepper
- Vegetable oil
- 2 boneless pork chops

Katsudon
- 1 teaspoon tsuyu sauce
- 2 eggs
- 2 tablespoon soy sauce
- 1 tablespoon sugar
- 2 tablespoon sake
- 2 tablespoon mirin

- 100ml water
- 1 large white onion

Method:

1. To begin, cook rice in a pressure cooker with liquid.
2. Season all sides of the pork chop with salt and black pepper.
3. To begin, flour both sides of the beef.
4. Soak them in a mixture of egg and milk.
5. Position the coated chicken breasts in the oil cautiously and bake for four minutes on either side or until lightly browned.
6. Combine the rest of the ingredients and stir well.
7. When the onions are loosening, break two eggs into a mixing bowl and whisk them together.
8. In the same pan, insert the katsu and the egg.
9. Allow for 1-2 minutes of cooking time.
10. Serve with chopped green onion or your favorite greens as a garnish.

69

CALIFORNIA SUSHI ROLLS

Cooking Time: 1 hour
Serving Size: 64
Ingredients:
- 1 medium ripe avocado
- Reduced-sodium soy sauce
- 1 small cucumber
- 3 ounces imitation crabmeat
- 2 cups sushi rice
- Bamboo sushi mat
- 8 nori sheets
- 2 cups water
- 2 tablespoons sesame seeds
- 2 tablespoons black sesame seeds
- ¼ cup rice vinegar
- ½ teaspoon salt
- 2 tablespoons sugar

Method:
1. Merge rice and water in a big frying pan and set aside for thirty minutes.
2. Get the water to a boil. Cover and set aside for ten minutes.

3. In the meantime, whisk together the vinegar, syrup, and salts in a shallow saucepan until the sugar dissolves.

4. Drizzle the vinegar solution over the rice in a wide shallow dish.

5. Place aside the toasted and black sesame seeds on a tray.

6. Put ¾ cup rice on a piece of plastic wrap.

7. Place a tiny amount of cucumber, lobster, and avocado around 1-½ inches from the nori sheet's bottom side.

8. To make six rolls, repeat with the remaining components.

70

SUSHI BAKE CALIFORNIA MAKI

Cooking Time: 40 minutes
Serving Size: 20 portions
Ingredients:
Sushi Rice
- 1 tablespoon sugar
- 1 teaspoon salt
- 3 tablespoon rice vinegar
- 4 cups freshly cooked rice

Furikake
- 1 teaspoon salt to taste
- 1 teaspoon sugar to taste
- ½ cup Korean roasted seaweed
- ½ cup sesame seeds

Creamy Topping
- Salt to taste
- 20 sheets Korean seaweed sheets
- ¼ cup Japanese mayonnaise
- 1 tablespoon Sriracha
- 2 cups Kani shredded
- 200 grams cream cheese

- 1 medium cucumber
- 1 big ripe mango

Method:

1. In a small container, whisk together the rice wine vinegar, spice, and sugar.

2. Heat it in the oven until the sugar and salt have fully dissolved.

3. Toss the properly prepared rice with the combination until it is uniformly spread.

4. Mix the cream cheese, Japanese mayo, and Sriracha in a mixing dish.

5. Spread a thin layer of Fukikake over the rice until it is fully coated.

6. Layer the creamy topping uniformly on top.

7. Cook at 200°C for fifteen minutes.

CONCLUSION

A component of Japanese food is rice. It is also popular to eat rice cakes (mochi). They vary from savory to sweet and have many different methods, from grilled to boil. With heavy effects frcm both Korea and China, Japanese cuisine has been around for more than centuries. And it's only been several decades before all the results of what is now recognized as Japanese cuisine has begun to exist. Currently, the four seasons and climate also have a significant influence on Japanese food. Most frequently, fish and veggies are consumed. Although the food may sound almost ordinary to some western people, tastiness, appearance, and combination of flavors are of utmost importance. This book has all types of Japanese dishes categorizing into breakfast, snacks, lunch, dinner, soups, and some of the famous recipes of Japanese cuisine. Try these recipes and start preparing your easy and delicious Japanese meals.

Milton Keynes UK
Ingram Content Group UK Ltd.
UKHW021506230824
1366UKWH00042B/371